A Late Night and a Third Bourbon

A Late Night and a Third Bourbon

A Herbert Ashe

A Herbert Ashe
2014

First Printing: 2014

ISBN 9780692702420

www.anthonyherbertashe.com

To you?…

Contents

Love.

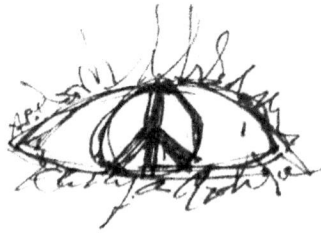

10

<u>Let Her Be Beautiful</u>
For herself
Holding so much back
For you

Let her be beautiful
Like
Her favorite color
Or song
And the tree she loves to sit beneath
Or climb

Let her be beautiful
Since
She belongs to no one
Though
You treat her like property
Your property

Let her be beautiful
Because
Gorgeous will never tell the story

Let her be beautiful
You know she deserves it
Imperfect
Of course
But
So are we

Let her be beautiful
Because
Tears look awful
Under such peaceful eyes

Let her be beautiful
Because
If you've seen her move
The way I have
You know she is no longer giving her best

Let her be beautiful
She will be better at everything
When
Her mind is clear

Let her be beautiful
As wonderful as she seems
She is destined for more
When freed of misery

Let her be beautiful
Making her wait any longer
Suffocates us all

Let her be beautiful
The setting sun looks for her
At the river's edge
Missing their synergy
I saw it once
It has no equal

Let her be beautiful
The time of her life
Didn't last long enough

You Are Who You Are
A giraffe should never have to thank me
For treating it like a tall animal

I suppose I could pretend
To be
In the presence of a dog
But
Life is so much easier
If I am honest

Never thank me for telling the truth

Laugh at the liars
And
Those who do not see you for who you are

Remember It
There was a moment
When it was all really good
And
Every thought became a poet's dream
And
They danced together without regret
And
They begged for rain with every passing cloud

They loved every song

16

Just Drown
You have been so ready
For so long
Too long
Treading water
Looking and waiting
For
That arm
To reach down
So
Your tired legs
Strong
But
Oh so tired
Can stop saving you from sinking

You're Back
When that face
Comes around that corner
That
Sharp corner
My bones dance
Beneath my skin
Trying hard to contain myself

<u>Faking It</u>
Funny
They all know
So do we
You and I
And
Everyone else
Fake nothing
Make everything
Love

<u>It</u>
It was always
Number one
We knew it
From the first minute
Through
The fifth hour

<u>I Knew</u>
I knew when I saw your face
I would see you
Forever
Thank you for making me
Look
Brilliant

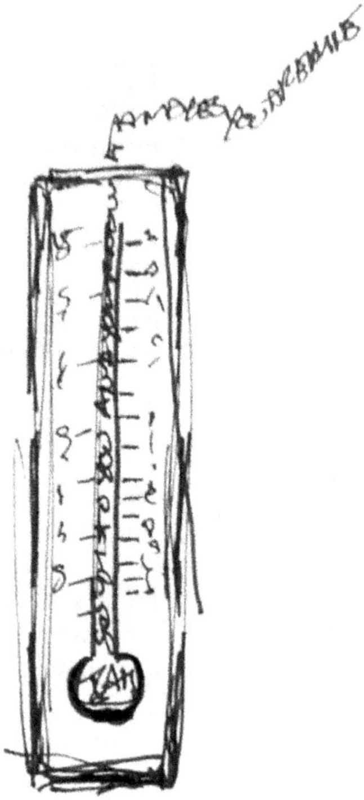

Humid August

In a nasty
You know it
So does anyone
Everyone
Who sees the way I am
looking

In a nasty
My hands are sweaty
Drying them
On the top sheet
You don't notice

In a nasty
Eyes looking up
At something
Every ten seconds

In a nasty
It might hurt
In a few hours
I don't care if you don't

In a nasty
Someone should call
Time out
For this kind of scoring
streak

In a nasty
The hunger
You brought in
Will be back
As soon as you leave

In a nasty
I will never look
At that spot
The same way
Again

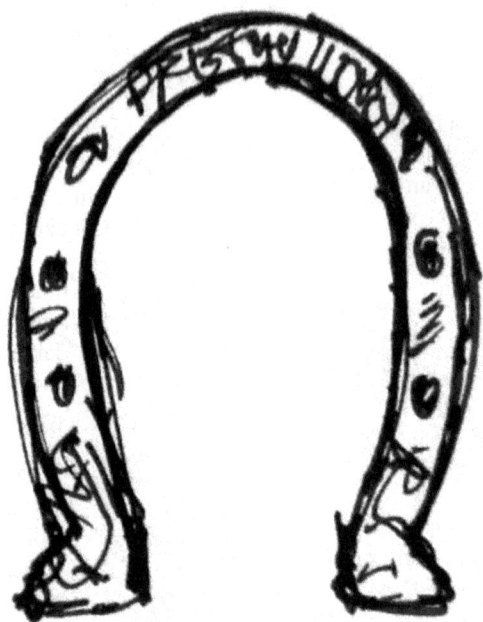

<u>The Most Beautiful</u>
I have seen
My eyes have seen many

Only seen

Still
The most beautiful
You may disagree
I will not waver
Convinced
Completely
If you challenge my belief
Keep it quiet
Leave me
Ignorant and happy
Feeling lucky

<u>Truth</u>
Make someone you love
Do something they hate
To keep you
As happy as
You can be
And
See how long
You can keep
Saying you love them
While seeing a sad woman
A very sad woman
Across the table
And
A liar in the mirror

<u>Picturing Lovely</u>
Without freckles
Singing
That one is between X
And why
Trouble
She is reckless with hearts
Made of silver
And
Laces that long to be tied

<u>Higher</u>
Than this or you
Above your peaks
Squinting to see them
High
So high
No one sees me
They see you
They admire
Necks break below your pedestal
I am still
Looking
Hard

Early Morning Grace
Pure white feathers
Blowing
In underground tunnels
Right past the rest of you
And
Onto my shoulder

I stare for far too long
Then
Send it on its way
Lucky me

Hesitant and Lonely
She looks
But more importantly
She knows
Fixing her hair
In a dirty window
Looking
Until you do
She pauses
Ever so slightly
Before her eyes shift
Subtle smiles
Stares get longer
Alas
This is her stop
And
Not yours

Better Days
Too many Thursdays
Give way to free Fridays
No
Expectations
Anxiety
Lying
In wait
For promise
Redemption

Glimpses of heaven
Come
And go

Talentless
Bleeding fingers
Of
A bad guitar player
Out of tune
No rhythm
Plays all the same
Hardly
But
Passionately

AND AGAIN   I WILL LOVE YOU
             TO THE MOON
             AND BACK   AND AGAIN

30

<u>I Felt</u>
Great
One day
Smiles stuck on my welcoming face
Sunshine
Pierced my lips
Absorbed
Circulating with every beat
Looked at my hands
I saw the happiness
Moving
Flowing

Enjoying
Mutually
One day was
Great
Let us speak of the rest tomorrow

<u>On a Brick</u>
In the wall
Of an old Knoxville office
He wrote

"I will love her to the moon and back"

I stared for a minute
Then felt bad for the poor guy
Still on lap 1

<u>It Only Comes Once</u>
To the lucky
Never
To many
Too many
To live without it
Caves
Filled with sawdust
Instead of stone
Water
Tears
Will wash it away
Left to echo
Echo echo
You had it once
Confidently let it go
Fully expecting
To receive it again

<u>Revelation</u>
You had
No idea
You had
Never made it
Until
You made it with me
And
All of those butterflies
Flew in
Concentric circles
Fluttering still
Only now
In sync
Don't thank me
I didn't know either

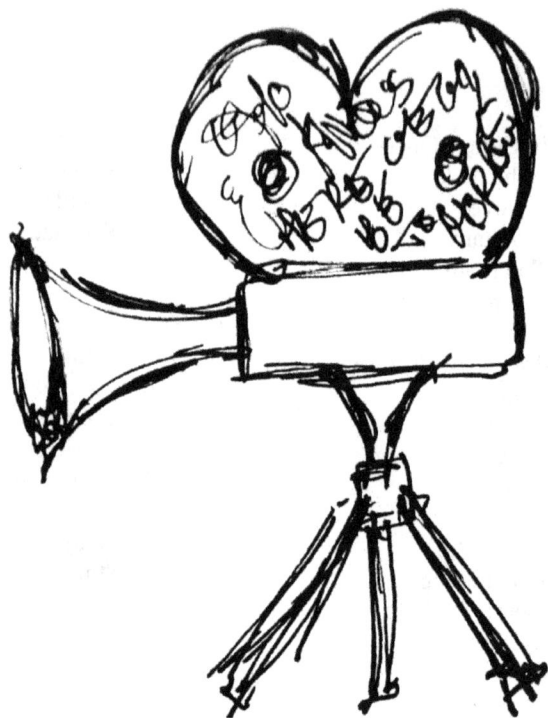

Lights Flicker

Between trunks
of trees
I am moving
Fast
To a place I hate
Full of empty
progress
And
Far from my
cares
Those lights
flicker
I am moving

Not forward

Infatuation

Blanket me
wholly
Feet to neck

Leave my face
Uncovered

So I can see you

Refresh

From a time
When
All was right
And
Joy bulged
through our
chests
Here
You were
Eyes locked
Conquered
world
Movie worthy
No credits

Wrong Time

When that rage
So abundant
Is contained
Bottled in a soul
Trying its best to be peaceful
That red
Dark red
Bloody Red
Will find its way past
That bright yellow filter
Splashing against
The unfortunate object
Finding itself in the wrong
place

You

There has always been
Something about you
Hidden
Beneath that prudence
Hoping to be bigger
Than the present allows

Touch My Face

In the rain
Eyes of admiration
Staring hard
Wet hand
And
Cheek
United
Under the umbrella
Tears not raindrops
Eyes
Still
Stare

ALL YOU WILL
EVER NEED
IS RIGHT HERE
WAITING

PAY ATTENTION

<u>Working it Out</u>
That arm
So strong
Impressive

Handing out more
Headlocks than hugs
Choking
What it should be sharing
Because it learned
Never to expose
More than it can defend
Love left it weary
So now
Every embrace
Protects

<u>Standing</u>
On the dark highway
I see
Only white lights

Turn to see
The red
Hop to the side
Surprise me

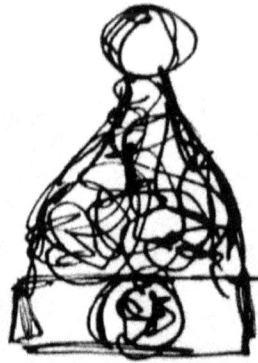

Matching Hats
Puffy and Warm
Matching hearts
(see above)

Dreams
That might not be
Dreams
That never will

Wake up smiling

Perfect
The hair
The sun
The set
All
So right

Also left

And even in having to walk away

I could not have planned a more perfect day

<u>Anonymity</u>
Super man
Trace this
Find this
Find me
Keeper
I am the crier
Not you
All together and shit
Looking sane
Looking good
For
The camera with no film

<u>Evoke</u>
Some
Thing
From you
Hurts when you speak
Blankly
Generic smile
We know
What you hide
Deep away
Show it
Or
Lose it

Forever.

44

<u>She Came Looking</u>
For answers she already knew
With
Unpainted toes
And
A skirt that feels like a t-shirt
To the touch
To the knees
To
The knees
It will flow in the breeze
If there is one

Still

Wasting her time on things she knows
Trying
Desperately
To leave a smile on a frowning face
Before that breeze
Blows her skirt up
And
Blows her away

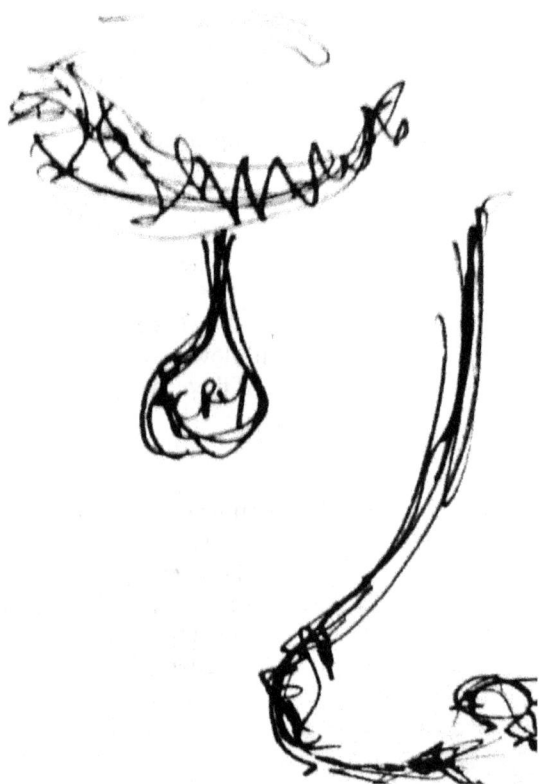

Red Lights

Flash
Pulsate
Even when the train isn't
coming
Slow pace then a brief delay
Air is stagnant
Even when the wind blows
Through
These deep dark tunnels
Red lights pulsate
Flash
They don't know any better

Thorough Lies

Smoke screens
She walks right
Through
To your guilty
Face
Sorry for yourself
Selves
Reasons diverge
But
Sad is sad
Everyone cries together

Brown Rose

Resting above your ear
Secure
In the simple braid
Innocent face around lovely
eyes
One man looks down your
shirt
Yet another
Peeking between your seated
thighs
Making a father thankful
For sons

Some of Those Friends
A few of those ladies
The one you married
A couple of others
Look them in the eyes
Especially one
Tell her
What
You told us
No one
With
Feet still planted
On
Natural ground
Knows pearls that lovely
Gates that tremendous

Smile and dance
Mambo if you like

Life Goes
On and off
Same desk
Work
Passwords
But
Pictures
Turn homage to memorial

Please don't ask
How
I am doing

Don't Console Me
Uninspired apologies
No cliché comfort
Or
Textbook tact
Works
When all you can think of
Is
That day
And
How light you slept
And
How the call was no surprise
And
You couldn't decide when to cry
And
You walked in the dark of night
And
The moon was asking for him
And
You didn't want to arrive
But you did
And
You made the room worse
With
Your uncontrollable tears

<u>Heaven</u>
For a lost love
Find her
In the clouds

When the rain stops
We will know
You found her

We will all look

To the sun

To

The son

And start to smile

Smile again

Just as you would want us to

<u>Misunderstood</u>
Brilliance
Will not
Always
Manifest itself in ways that please
The people around you

A superior mind
Is
Uncontrollable
A burden when trapped
In a mismatched existence

They
All of them
Misunderstand your need
Your need to be numb

Genius
Flying in circles
Will crash
In an ocean of insanity

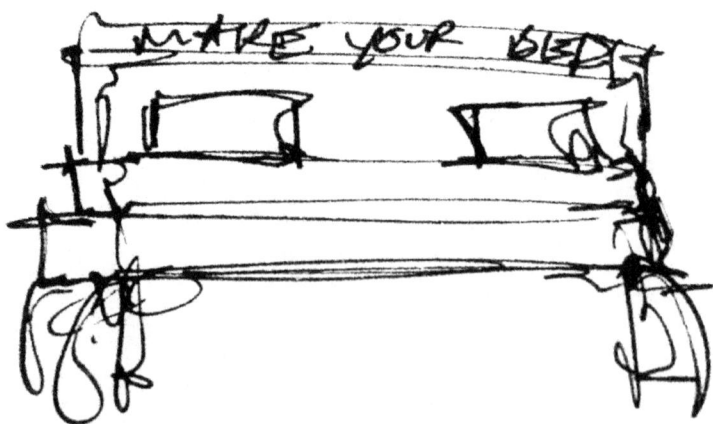

Cold Waiting
Tap my feet
Until I cry
It ain't dancing
And
You ain't singing
Well
Perhaps you are
But
I can't hear you
Nowhere near you
Or
Your pillows
All of them
Neatly placed
Stacks and rows
And
Cold
Very Cold

Lay down and stop pretending

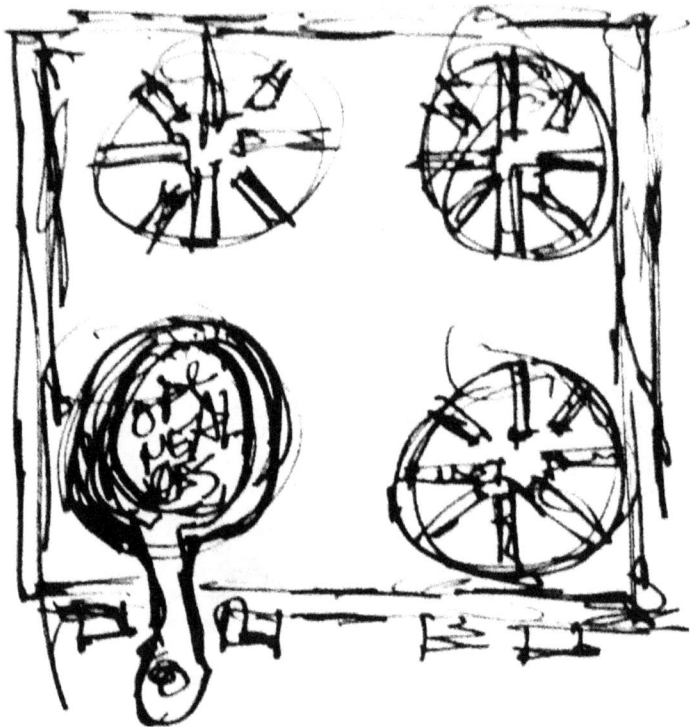

Too Many Chatty Mornings

Not so bright
Please
Spare my eyes
Not so untrue
Spare white lies

Too Many Nights
Alone on a couch
Only
One eye working
Book of matches
And
Simmering oatmeal
Surrounded by pictures
Of
Family
And
Loves lost
Long ago

Wake up and see them

Remembering Things
I should not have to
Do you have to remember
The palm of your hand?

Turn it over
Refresh

But
I am remembering things
I should not have to
Do you have to remember
The price of milk?

Tags
Clearly marked
Visible

Still
I am remembering things
I should not have to

I should not
Have to
Remember things
Things that are supposed to be
Right in front of me

I remember you

<u>That Genius</u>
Lost
In the junk drawer
Blindly digging
Pricking fingers
Nothing but pain
Found
Dump it all
On the floor
Watch it disappear

<u>Crossroads</u>
After every step
More decisions
Notches
On my trusty walking stick
Counting
Running out of
Wood
Mental capacity
Care
For any of you
Except them

<u>Synergy</u>
Worlds converge
And
Build the amazing
Not perfect
But
Undoubtedly amazing

Decent Posture
There you stood
Full of love
Knowing you were wrong

You still are

Gorgeous
As always
Too right
To be anything but
Crying

The Only Reason
We all hope
Pray
Allow ourselves to love
Are for moments
Like this
When our eyes gaze on fuel
For rapidly beating hearts

Stranded
It never hurts
As much as it hurts
When I am staring at blank
canvas
Alone
Music dancing between my
ears
Brush in my hand
Paralyzed
Come and get me

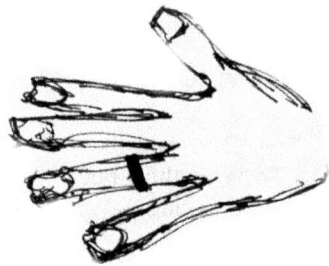

<u>Stuttered Vow</u>

I

I

I

ha ha ha

haven't know

know know

known

ma ma much

Love

in n in

thi thi thi thi this

lie lie lie lie lie life

of of of

my my my

mine

buh buh but

wa wa when

I

I

I

ma ma ma met

ya ya you

I

I

I

I

na na knew

my my my

Love

Could not be any stronger

Open is…
As open does
Exposed and hurt
Constant vulnerability
Waiting
For validation that never comes
Toasting to
Your own accomplishment
With one glass
Plenty of refills

Solitude
A figment of my imagination
If a figment
Can be great
This one certainly is

Imaginary
I threw
It through you
I thought
You were translucent
Or
Shallow
I had no idea
You were a mirage

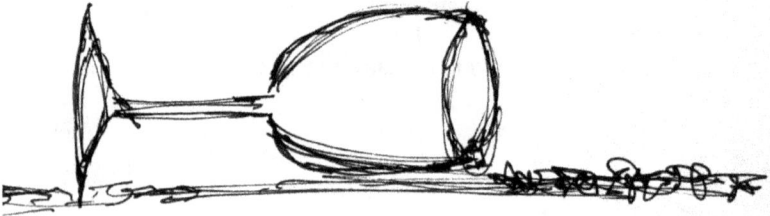

Life.

<u>Constant Inspiration</u>
Every phrase is a masterpiece
When
You write from a place
No one else will ever know
Unless you tell them
And
You love it
In a way
That makes your face red
And
Your head light
And
Your mind right
And
Your fingers numb

The pen falls

Right through your useless hands

Reminding you to drink

Eat

Breathe

And

Keep going

Are You Dead?
If life loses
The element of surprise
And
Every moment is
Part of the routine
And
The world can set its clock
To you
And
White sauce on pasta is variety
And
Everyone knows it

If
You can write a song to your own pulse
And
The song is never off beat

Don't even bother

Dying
Trying to be
The happiest man
On
Any street
But
Working this hard
When
It could be so easy
Is
Taking its toll
Especially since I never succeed

74

All of This
Running and dodging
For
Trains that may not be the right color
And
May be leaving
Instead of arriving
Does not bother me

As much as the faces
The miserable faces
Who live and die
Seem to live
And
Die
By
The "Just made its"
And
"Barely missed its"

Footsteps
The way
We walked
The way we ended up here
So gone
So quickly
Loud crashes
Strong waves
Stealing all traces
Dragging them away

Nothing left to guide you
Unless of course
You remember

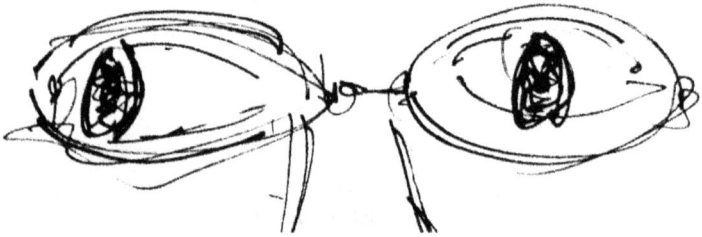

<u>Flutter</u>
Those words
Bring back the butterflies
From
Old nights
And
New love
When
We would pass out
Trying to put each other to sleep

I am wide awake
But
I don't have to be

<u>Hindsight</u>
I fell in love
So deep
So deeply
With that lazy-eyed woman
I thought
It wandered for only me
In every waking moment
She gave me the attention
I felt
I deserved
Or
So it seemed

<u>My Dreams are Still</u>
Vivid
And still
I find it difficult to convince myself
That
You are real

Many people
With
Minds lost
Believe in deceptive senses
Unable to feel
Any other reality
I could be making you up
Making everyone up
In response to mental trauma
I no longer recall

But

My tears have always been wet

What You Are

You are not my heart
Not even close
You
Are like that thing
In
That superhero's chest
The metal one
With
The shrapnel stuck in his body

The magnet
The electromagnet
That is you
To me

That thing
That vital thing
Keeping that shrapnel
From destroying me

When you are in
I am alive
I am well

When you are out
I am alive
But
Not for long

<u>Beef Stew</u>
Fed to me
From her
Spoon
Pot
Stove
Disgust
Verge of vomit
Faucet dripping
Twisting and turning
Helplessly
No flow
But
She keeps spooning it out
And
Stuffing it in
I look into her eyes
And
Keep smiling

Anticipating dessert

Who, Me?
I told the world what I
thought
It wanted to hear from me
Every time
Every single time
A question was asked

Everyone just knew who I
was
And
What I would be

Now
Their respect for the real me
Is
A bittersweet surprise

I could have been me a long
time ago

IBIWISY
You say you are
Finished with that
Ready for this
I'll believe it when I see you

You say you are
Preparing
Making
Moving
Shaking
I'll believe it when I see you

You say you have
New hair
New glasses
New body
New attitude
I'll believe it when I see you

You say you are
Ready to
Give
Miss
Love
…

Finding You

Here it comes
Plowing through all obstacles
Crashing through everything
in its path
Computers
Paper
Canvas
Metal
Wood
Hitting houses
Huge houses
Without slowing down

The truth is a heat seeker
And
You are hot
Hot indeed

Dream On

Vivid dreamer
Practically crippled
Since
Most artists are starving
And
You like to eat
And
Your things are nice

They are so nice

And
You want more
So much more than
Real love

Do without it
Keep the rest
Sit on your material
mountain
Let it slide
Let you slide

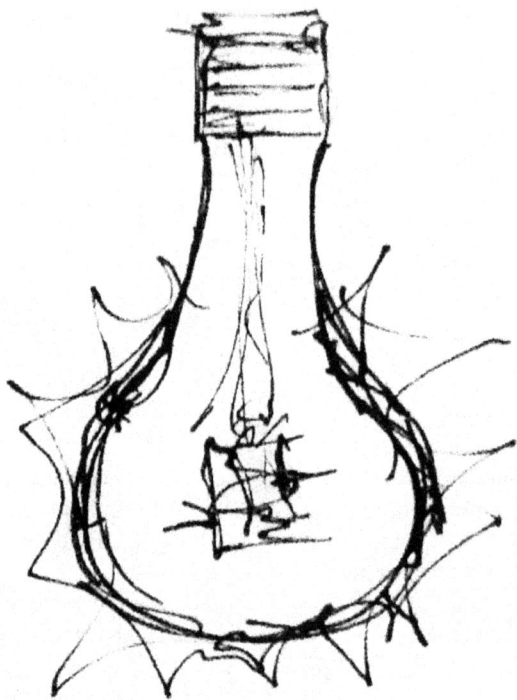

<u>Mirage</u>
I run my hands along my fantasy
Knowing what it is
Yet
Hoping it will jump into reality
I keep touching
Dreaming
Eyes wide
Winking
Enjoying the flashes

<u>Tricky Eyes</u>
I have spent far too much
Of life
Running after red circles
I see when
I stare at light bulbs
A better set of hands
Perhaps

<u>I Am Awake</u>
Painless nights
Spent
In wonderful dreams
Betrayed by my alarm

<u>Homecoming</u>
When I was back home
The faces were familiar
And
The walls were still blue
And
The reservoir was still full
And
My jump shots still fell
On
The playground courts
But
The bullies have lost their teeth
And
There are no more crushes on old squeezes
And
The young parents are all great
Grand

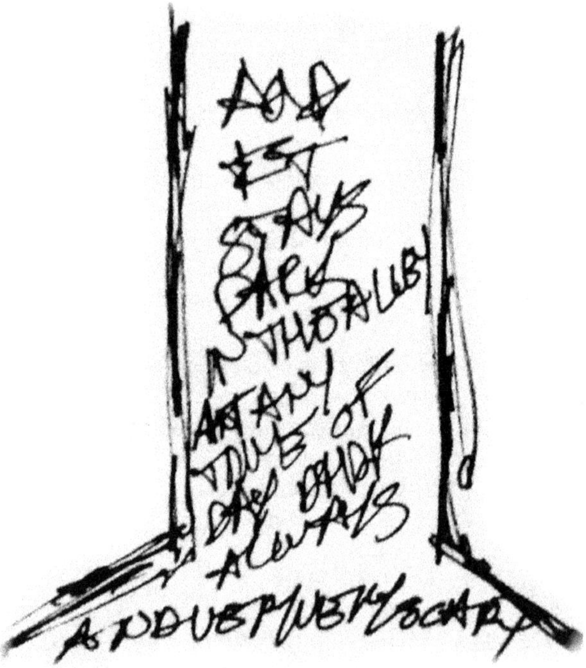

They Aren't All Bad
There are days
Some days
When
The best is relative
And
You can smile at everything
And
The mile seems shorter
And
Feet feel like pillows no matter how hard I stomp
Though
On days like this
I don't do much stomping

One Last Anxious Chance
Waiting
In an alley
Partially lit
But
An alley nonetheless
With
No plan B
No alternative seems reasonable
Pushing buttons
Nothing changes
Remotely

I've been here before
In the dark
The pain seemed endless
Those flickering lights
Are
Unnerving

<u>No Longer Looking for Myself</u>
I have been found
Safe and sound
But
I fear
There may not be another person
For miles

Wait

There she is
Hiding her face
Her
Stunning face
In a patch of sunflowers
Tall sunflowers
And
That rustling in the field
Behind her
It is them
The two of them
Running in circles

Clipped Wings
All of them
The ones you know
Conspiring
Night and day
In their spare time
To keep you
Yes you
Stuck on the tarmac
Grounded
Strapped in
With
No hope for flight

Blame them
All of them
For
Having nothing
Absolutely nothing
Better to do with their time
You should be there
Up there
Hovering between clouds and stars
Soaring in a heavenly breeze
Guarding the thin line between
Living and Blessing

GOODBYE
FATE THAT I NEVER CHOSE

Indelible Images
Waves of rejection
Are
What they are
Because
You never stay
When you should

You know you should

We hug
Hello
And
We wave
Goodbye

Goodbyes
Feel so wrong
So
Inadvertently hurtful

I remember the hand
Instead of the face

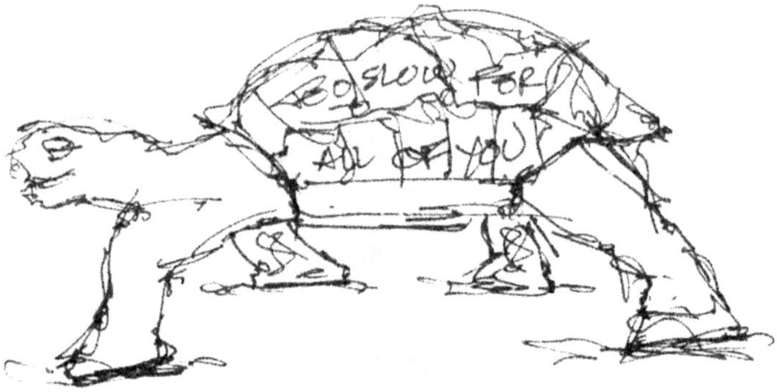
SLOW FOR
ALL OF YOU

<u>Some Times</u>
Some
Times
There is nothing to say
Yet
I find myself
Fighting against words
Prying my lips open

Some
Times
I wish for an empty mind
A tortoise
In a land
Where
Rabbits are extinct
Or
They appear to be
And
Somehow manage to hide
Among the majority

Some
Times
Sometimes
Is not good enough

<u>So What?</u>
Black eyes
Swollen and tender
I should have ducked
Broken knuckle
Hurts whenever it moves
Stupid me for swinging
Blindly
Sore elbow from trying to brace my fall
Scraped knees
When I struggled
To my feet
Cracked ribs from the kicks
But
What a fight it was

104

One Side
Every story seems logical
Sensible
Believable
When replayed during sleepless nights

A kind heart
Hoping for truth and peace
Might be inclined to take one shoe
Put it on and go for a walk
Pretending to be
Wearing a pair
But
That second shoe
Might make you realize
How long you have been limping

So Far
The best we can do is
Getting so close
So very close
That every word
Every single word
Seems like an item in a shopping cart
Instead of a wish list

<u>If You See Me</u>
If you ever
See me
With puffy eyes
Puffy red eyes
Don't walk over
With that face
That
Empathetic face
To put your hand on my shoulder

I cry
I cry
I cry tears of joy
More often than
I weep
In sadness

So
If you see me
If you ever
See me
Crying
Just smile
Tilt your head
Ever so slightly
And
Leave me alone

And
Don't call me a liar

Forest
Ends at an open field
Grass a vibrant green
The sun seems like
Heaven calling
It exists
And
So do we
Sitting
Basking
The wind between the blades is soothing
Like
A lullaby from Grandma
Wishing for paralysis
It never comes
Limbs are all functional
The wind sings louder
I know I have to go

An Old Man's Winter Wisdom
Every once in a while
When it gets really cold
The ice must be cracked
And
Kicked down stream
Or
Your boat will never move

Fragile Peace
Cracking under the weight
The considerable weight
Of
Chaos
And
Human nature
Peace does not suffocate
It disappears

Another Dream
There is a place
Not too far
But
Very much away
From this
Where
Her next smile only needs an open eye
And
Dances never end
At sunset
And
The sand is never too hot

Bodies are like hands
Holding each other

Your Eyes Smile
Always smiling
Even
When your face refuses to cooperate
And
You are afraid to emote

No one blames you
The hat's brim
Will
Conceal your mood
When
Your head is down
But
When you look up
Oh
When you look up

Those eyes
They radiate
All
Though
You are scared to make the rest of you
Match them

If you change your life
To
Match your eyes
You may lose
All you have acquired
And
If you change your eyes
To
Match your life
You may lose
What you have always been

114

Mr. Happy
Such power
Elegance
I am humbled by the sound of you

Unbelievable
Better than
I ever expected
Real smiles abound

The season for those
Has passed
I suppose

Gone

I nailed that smile onto my face
So deep
The metal is no longer visible
But
If I make sudden moves
I can still feel them

116

<u>Feeling Better</u>
Look at you
All
Neat
And
Tidy
With
Your shoulders curled back
Looking proud

They are looking again
You know it
Smile

<u>Louder</u>
Hear
In here
Than anywhere
You know

Toasting
Blackened
To everyone
Who is every one
In my book
Prolonging the prologue

Trying to begin
Too many
To acknowledge

Run on
Life
Sentences

Sketchbook
Hoping to be
Drawn
In or on
A part of the picture
In any
Capacity
Full of
Hope for it
Constantly

Gave
His money
To those it should go to
No need for it

Failed tests
On true priorities
Proven typical
Even after unique words
Told a conflicting story

Cried
Before he gave it away
Laughed
When it was gone

DONT TURN YOUR
BACK ON ME!!!!

122

<u>Spent</u>
Like a bowl full of change
Hands in constantly
Taking
Digging for the quarters
Eventually settling for
Nickels and dimes
Always leaving the pennies
Taking
Whenever necessary
Only replenishing
When
The sound of coins
Clanking against each other
Becomes a nuisance

That bowl of pennies
May be heavy
But
It is not worth much

Time to Book
When questions
Outnumber answers
And
Your face tells a sad story
Chapter after chapter
I hope you find a place to hide
And smile

Each Step
A lucky guess
Left to right
Left
To write
Owl necks
Twisting to see me
Stumble
Trip
Fall

LOCKED IN
BY CHAINS
BUT I'M DOING
JUST
FINE

<u>Symphony</u>
Coming into tune
Each instrument
Walking in
Preparing for perfection
Knowing
Why we are here

All of us
Needing
What they can easily give

We will all sit
We did not come here
To dance
Or
To sit in silence

<u>Some Thing</u>
Traps us
In the place
This place
Even
When happiness
Is clearly
So far
Far away

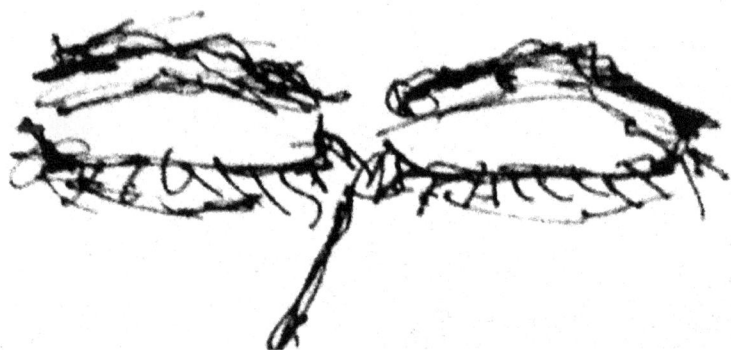

<u>I See the Light</u>
Above all else
Teasing my ignorance
Making my eyes hurt
Through every reflection
Clears
My drunken haze
When all I wish for
Is a few more moments
Of darkness
Closed eyes
Pleasant dreams

<u>Fate</u>
Seems like
The best possible dream
When luck
Always skips by
And
Persistence leads to frustration

Put me to sleep
Let fate have me
Because
Fighting anything
Takes energy
I no longer have to spare

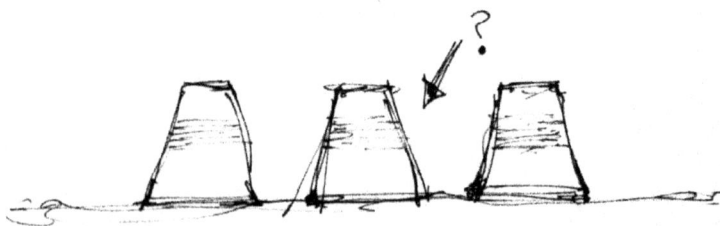

130

<u>Found</u>
Your facts
Your reality
Your
Decisions
In illusions
Cerebral
Treated to tricks
By every sense
Brought to tears
Mixed tears
Of
Joy and devastation
By reality
Yet
You
Make your choices
Based on mirages
And
Parlor tricks
Designed
Specifically
To make you think
Happiness is in the middle cup
When
It has already been put in your back pocket

<u>Second Chances</u>
What might have been
Now
Lost
In the hands
Of a first night waiter
Waiting
For later
What could have been
Found
Never was
No one looked
What might have been
Wrong
Because
Time will do that
To right
What might have been
Lost
In the shuffle
Of
Love and practical thinking
What might have been
Trapped
In a book
On a shelf
No one can reach
What might have been
Forgotten
Like the name
Of that song
It goes like this

What a Time We Had
Memorable by any standard
Perfect by our own
Far from trouble
Or
The clutches of the world around us

We chased every smile
And
Caught quite a few
Enough to make those we missed seem distant
Insignificant

In years to come
We will talk as if we caught them all

Perhaps we did
Perhaps we still are

Noblewoman
How heroic of you
To endure
Life in a cage
Welded at the corners
Fed well
While
Putting up with put downs
I guess
Knowing you cannot leave
Makes it all easier
Even if that cage is all you will ever get

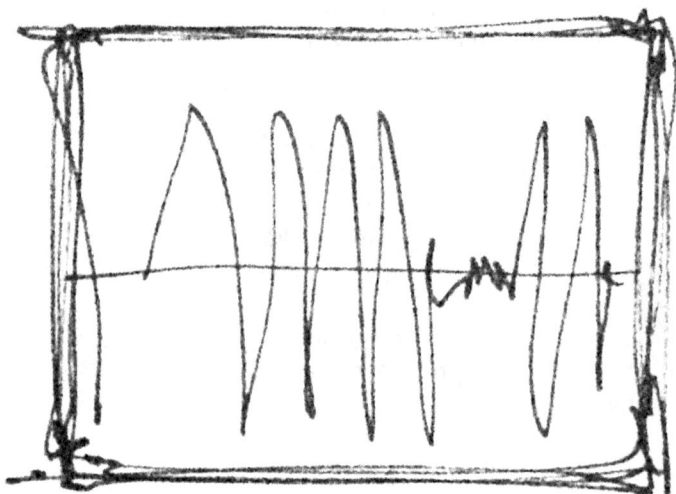

<u>Still Alive</u>
Still
Alive for you

When

Death seems to be firing
Over
My unsuspecting head
And
All grass looks brown
Both sides
And
War is always
Instead of sometimes
And
The only people not taking
Are protecting what they have

I am more alive
Alive for you
Than ever

<u>Life and…</u>
There are times
When
The sighs seem more frequent
Than
The breaths between
And
The word itself
Between
Seems too frequently said
To be anything less
Than
My middle name

There are times
When
Nothing is left
In the reflection
Or
The projection
For you to be
Proud of
And
All that is left to say to anyone is

"Live your life – it is all that is truly yours."

www.ingramcontent.com/pod-product-compliance
Lightning Source LLC
Chambersburg PA
CBHW060017050426
42448CB00012B/2795